STELLAR

poems by

Esther Lim Palmer

Finishing Line Press
Georgetown, Kentucky

STELLAR

FOR MY FAMILY

Copyright © 2021 by Esther Lim Palmer
ISBN 978-1-64662-714-1 First Edition
All rights reserved under International and Pan-American Copyright Conventions. No part of this book may be reproduced in any manner whatsoever without written permission from the publisher, except in the case of brief quotations embodied in critical articles and reviews.

ACKNOWLEDGMENTS

These poems first appeared, sometimes in slightly modified form, in the following literary journals and anthologies:

Brief Wilderness: "The Binding Bee"
Brushfire Literature and Arts Journal: "Happy New Year (Audio Guide to Alcatraz)"
California Quarterly: "Free"
Plainsongs: "Imagination at Reverie Lake"
Poetry in the Time of Coronavirus, Volume Two: "Spring 2020"
Westwind: "Inside"

Publisher: Leah Huete de Maines
Editor: Christen Kincaid
Cover Art and Design: Dusan Arsenic
Author Photo: Aika Cardin

Order online: www.finishinglinepress.com
also available on amazon.com

Author inquiries and mail orders:
Finishing Line Press
PO Box 1626
Georgetown, Kentucky 40324
USA

Table of Contents

Free 1
Spring 2020 2
Fallen Rain 3
Imagination at Reverie Lake 4
The Wait 5
Playing Pretend 6
Sun-Bleached Sand Dollar 7
Haves & Nots 8
All the Colors 9
White-Blue Haiku 10
The Binding Bee 11
Evergreen 12
Flicker 13
A Bunny 14
Switch 15
Ghazal in the Year Twenty-Twenty 16
Stellar 17
Rainbow Prism 18
5 AM, Again 20
White Noise 21
Believe 22
Inside 23
Prodigal Fish 24
De Minimis 25
Happy New Year (Audio Guide to Alcatraz) 26
Tomorrow 27
Morocco 20XX 28
Wolves Howl, Good Night 29
Beautiful 30

*O my soul, do not aspire to
immortal life, but exhaust the limits of the possible.*
—*PINDAR*

FREE

I should, myself, now sink to sleep,
When lamb is slumbering, at last,
And tiger, too, is tamed and warm.

I should, myself, now sink to sleep,
But a hairline moon fractures the night,
And with curled finger beckons me.

Come out, it urges. Only you, alone.
Only you, yes, you, alone. So I tiptoe
To open the midnight door and release

A sliver of self. And a breeze—crisp
And new—swiftly unlocks my lips, with keys
That free all my cells. Then it leaves me be

With the moon in this phase—two slivers
Of light this night—unfazed and free, silent
And free, simply being this nothing night.

SPRING 2020

Shifting sands stretch far, street after desolate street.
I do not know when the rising heat will subside;
When it will be cool to step outside again.

Sometimes the sun shifts a small shadow into view—
Another person, perhaps? Or perhaps nothing
But another mirage. Solitude starts to see things.

Lately, the wind leaves words outside the window
Cracked open; words like invisible gifts.
Comforting: This ambiguous loss will be over soon.

Questioning: And when it is over, what will I
Remember, and what will I too soon forget?
Reminding: Yes, there is sand here. But water too;

Inside, an oasis if I stop now to dig, and drink.
Not as a dog digs with a mouthful of bone
(I have no-one to hide my secrets from this hour).

But rather, another primal unearthing—a desire to dig
And dig, to find the why of life with gifted time;
Weeding out noxious want, and filling cupped hands

Only with nourishing need. This, I fear I will forget
When it is all over—the source of many springs—
That which sustains a quenching, blue-green reality.

FALLEN RAIN

you recall
another / downcast
afternoon / a lone
window / left
open /

you recall / finding me
there / pressing small
psalms / on a tensile
screen / still
wet / with rain /

you recall / the unsurprised
willow / outside /
that seemed / to lift
and nod / its knowing
head / looking up /

and in / not to miss
this moment / to have
and to hold / fallen rain /

IMAGINATION AT REVERIE LAKE

I

Sometimes,
I see it: early morning egret wings forging
through the fog—languid, lowering,
lifting. Then slender legs, two
guiding lines, center into view,
and wait upon that dewy log.
Bittersweet scent of coffee.
Wings flick, head
sways. Egret
flits.

Away.

II

Weeks, I wait. Weeks,
watching from the blind.

Hush. Here it comes again.

III

Awake
it rests in Reverie Lake.
Head gently bowed and eyes
softly closed as though in invocation.
Then slowly, it moves with widening wings
and dips its smooth beak into the light—to go
awhile into itself. Celestial circles swirl.

THE WAIT

Comes
and goes,
as she pleases.

Does she know how I wait
for her?

How the whole lake waits,
and life chills—still
waiting
for her return.

PLAYING PRETEND

I lay my body long on spades of sand.
I let my fingers link beneath my head.
I lower my eyes and listen to you play.

You lay your little body next to mine.
Your pinkies link and twirl your sun-kissed curls.
You blink then squint to hear the deep green sea.

To stay this way all day. To let the sea
Swell up and up, and bluff a lullaby.
As we all play pretend on the shore.

SUN-BLEACHED SAND DOLLAR

Worth what in death?
No longer a home.
Nothing to hold fast.
Dormant ornament,
At best. Some value
For a moment
When remembered.
Then returned to the shelf—
A photo fixed in a frame.
At least I have company here.
Conch, will you come closer?
And remind me of life at sea.
Roar of an open ocean,
Light from a boundless sky.
Those broken waves—salty
And receding on the shore.
High tide, low tide.
Over and again.
It's not that I thought
It would never end.
A precious life over
There, there.

HAVES & NOTS

The orange moon is ripe
and glows low
for the picking.

Fingertips of midnight mist
peel off
smooth citrus skin.

And down below,
broken streetlights flicker
with quivering lips

desperate
for just one lick
of that juicy illusion.

ALL THE COLORS

What color was the room?
    Sunburst yellow.

What color was the dragonfly?
    Electric blue.

What color was curiosity?
    All the colors of the rainbow.

What color was fear?
    Blood red.

What color crawled out in reverse?
What color forced the door shut?
    What color can stop a start down darkness?

WHITE-BLUE HAIKU

i.
White rabbit in snow—
Oh, the possibilities!
Sitting down to write.

ii.
Darkness bore a dove.
It trilled like a light blue flute—
Youthful notes of hope.

iii.
Shiny blue button
Rolls off the old woman's coat.
Long white thread holds on.

iv.
Sea slips in and out.
Children gather skeletons—
Sun-bleached sand dollars.

THE BINDING BEE

Do we wake to wither, or climb
High for the rounded sky?
Must it be either?

I've grown in stillness—letting
Bumblebees sip my sweet nectar, and feeling
Their soft fur fill the hollow of my face
As they wiggle with natural contentment.
Here comes the rain again.

Let me not turn like autumn leaves,
Red and brittle with age,
Fallen and forgotten underfoot.

Let me live renewed in evergreen glades,
Among the hum of bees in the hive of bliss—
They will bring.

EVERGREEN

Where did you learn
To forge
Perfect circles,
Like that?
Another, beside another,
Just like that?

And you soak up the sunshine
And flirt with proud clouds, all
Wanting
To drench you
Evergreen.
To keep you
Blooming, so natural, it seems,
To fancy you
Alive
And forever
Green.

FLICKER

Running around, around and around,
she's all right with her golden ball—smooth
and round; all is shiny and round. And her wild,

open eyes catch the rising sun, as she throws
herself high through high bunny tail grass—
forgiving, soft, and warm. And there's

a springtime crown tightly tied with string,
soaring high with her streaming strands. Then,
snap: *Tag, you're it.*

Beauty fades, fast-forward.
Around and around, arms flailing around—
she falls and falls through all seasons; lands

deflated on damp, damned land. Would she beg
not to crawl through the winter? Rise again
to weather it all?

Should she spiral away in a blue, slipping light;
could she, somehow, remain soft and warm?
After fall, after fall—fight to flicker this night,
still forgiving, soft, and warm.

A BUNNY

bounded
across the yard,
three feet at a time.
Young, athletic, unafraid.

I missed
my marshmallow
burn and slip
off the stick.
Crooked and old.

Now it is eating my roses;
the red ones I planted
yesterday. It catches
my surprise without a flinch.
And just keeps nibbling.

SWITCH

You could
hide in a hole and pretend
nothing's happening. Blind,
like a subterranean mole rat.
But don't be daft— humans
don't hide. Do we?

Switch\
it off. I can't bear it any longer.

Wait, what did he say? Switch\
it back on, and start/stop/start
listening.
Everyone, switch!
Everything, on! Post
placards on windows, shut
down streets, march
with masses! What virus?

No, I said. Switch\
it off. I can't bear it any longer.

Don't make me look or listen anymore—
it's inhuman.
I used to sing in the shower.
Just want to be a mole
today.

Rats. Switch\

GHAZAL IN THE YEAR TWENTY-TWENTY

A gazelle lies conquered. The hyenas had fun.
Consent was implied, in the year twenty-twenty.

Blue knee, Black neck. A brother succumbs. The right
To breathe was denied, in the year twenty-twenty.

A killer is crowned. And swiftly spreads worldwide.
All locked inside, in the year twenty-twenty.

She rests in peace but remains alive. In laws
With pride, we abide, in the year twenty-twenty.

What did we say, when asked if things were okay?
Smiling, we lied, in the year twenty-twenty.

stellar

do
not fade
fearing
the night. hold tight
those constellations
no-one else
knows.
and for eternity shine bright
                unnamed.

RAINBOW PRISM

I have a map
to guide my body
back

home

where I'll bundle
into bed, and regress
to seed. Leaden legs
sink
into Mother Earth.

Yes, I forgot to take off
my coat. And yes, I suppose
I left
the door wide open, again—
sunlight streams in
like silence.
Everything
disappears to dust.

Room. Swoon.

Will you fill the void and sing me
to sleep? Old songs
refract all pain, soothing
strings like summer
Rain-
bow Prism, please, pierce through
this hueless heart—petals,

leaves.

I have a map. Still,
I can't place my mind.
And my body's
uprooted

again.

5 AM, AGAIN

In the bedroom, the baby is full
of sweet milk and sleep.

Behind the crib, the emptied
mother sits wide awake

rocking in the rocking chair
waiting for that rattle

of light's first light-rail to sound:
Please stand clear, doors closing.

WHITE NOISE

The newborn cannot sleep without it.
Then it learns to crawl, and climb, and question—
Scrambling to make sense
Of unintelligible distractions.
Two and three and four o'clock.
The impossible keeps us awake.

BELIEVE

All the lights go out
but one, by which
the mother soothes her child to sleep
with stories neither weary, nor worn.

But the mother's mind becomes lost
at the line from here
to disbelief; so the child, too,
lies—suspended—briefly

on this broken
bridge between. *Believe,*
reads the word in the book. (*I do,* once
vowed the mother.) *Believe,* sees the child.

INSIDE

Outside, Grandmother is fine
like china.
Inside, she feels sick—pain
pinpricking her stomach
for two days.
Outside, children are playing:
there's a gum-blowing competition
happening in the park, right now.
Inside, I want to be outside
playing too;
not here,
where a doctor is asking
me: *where does it hurt?*
Inside, I don't remember
the Korean word for stomach—only
the word for pain;
so Grandmother points to the pain.
Everyone understands pain.

PRODIGAL FISH

I swam
upstream
and caught
the eye
of an indifferent bear—
sat waiting
with entitled teeth;
miserable mouth gaped
open wide.

That bear didn't care
I'd grown
hooks and fangs,
a hump to jump,
help run; didn't care
I'd conquered
those undertows,
seeking streams;
sleepless streams—
take me home.

I swam
upstream
on rainbow scales
and caught
a slippery sun;
let it have me wholly—
an eternity,
it seemed, before
that brute was done.

DE MINIMIS

You,
who intrudes
on my mind; unwelcome
stranger—false friend
cloaked in cunning,
hiding behind
a wretched smile.

Show me
those hands you hide
in shallow pockets
empty
but for a few hapless hopes
that you sometimes
sneak out
to scatter a stench
for dirty dogs.

HAPPY NEW YEAR (AUDIO GUIDE TO ALCATRAZ)

Most haunting were not the walls that watched you
Stop by former stalls, framing memories,
Five feet by nine feet at a time.

Most haunting were not the names you saw beneath
Those steely eyes: Capone, Kelly, Cohen,
Karpis, The Birdman of Alcatraz, Young.

Have you ever lay in solitude by the Bay?
And could you hear that carrying chatter
From the shore? Echoes one cannot ignore.

Ever louder is the length of laughter.
Good folks ringing in a new year. Singing out
Those resolutions they intend to keep.

Most haunting was that Auld Lang Syne they could
Not escape from the Bay. How they tossed and turned,
They tossed, they turned. Another life away.

TOMORROW

She tries to translate
what this is
she has written.
To whom she has
long labored for.

But ink only bleeds
when truth spills
from her tongue.
Words can bruise,
words can bite like a brute.

So quickly she clicks
the fine point away.
Why? Click. Why? Click.
No more.

There's always tomorrow
to speak, she thinks.
Perhaps, tomorrow
to refine today.

MOROCCO 20XX

I wanted to stay
on that run-down rooftop,
where the sky burned orange
as the sound of prayer lifted
the air between you and me—
us, in this strange city.

I wanted to keep
every stray strand I'd stroked
and cut at your request,
on that run-down rooftop,
reluctantly snip-snipping
the hiss of summer away.

I wanted you
on that run-down rooftop,
with your back turned to me,
unmoving in a makeshift chair—
staring out, at something, then,
slowly, nothing, I couldn't see.

But the sky died down
as your locks fell free. And you
flew away
from that run-down rooftop
in that air still filled
with prayer.

WOLVES HOWL, GOOD NIGHT

Night—I say to you, is when
darkness drowns our bodies,
dragged down into quicksand
black—it happens so fast. No
time to breathe or reach
for that slippery
moon.

Night—you say to me, is when
we breathe (no, howl!). Howl
not up at the moon, but farther
out—beyond
vast valleys, despite
the darkness; deliberate
on all fours, howling: Come
to life; life
is green, life
is good.

Night—we say to you,
good night.

BEAUTIFUL

I shut my eyes
resenting the wings
I never asked for.
I grew used to
darkness—of feeling
enclosed. Layered away
from the world in a
womb. Safe. Connected.

If things don't work out,
they said, I could always
return. But everyone knows
it doesn't work that way.
Because once you're out,
you can never crawl back in—
no room for all
that baggage.

What I'm saying is,
something kicked my
chrysalis away. And cried,
you, the one with the wings,
you can't be here anymore.
Go find a new home.
Things have changed.
You're beautiful now.

Esther Lim Palmer was born in Sydney, Australia. To fulfill her South Korean immigrant father's wishes, she studied law at the University of Sydney, and practiced in Big Law for over a decade in Sydney, Hong Kong, and California. She is the author of the chapbook *Janus* (Finishing Line Press, 2020), and her work has appeared in various literary journals and anthologies, including *California Quarterly, Plainsongs, White Wall Review, Westwind, Poetry in the Time of Coronavirus, Volume Two, The Hungry Chimera, Brief Wilderness, Brushfire Literature and Arts Journal,* and *Oberon's Seventeenth Annual Issue*—selected to be archived in the EBSCO's Humanities' database for universities and cultural entities interested in contemporary literary work. She currently lives and writes in San Francisco.

www.ingramcontent.com/pod-product-compliance
Lightning Source LLC
LaVergne TN
LVHW040117080426
835507LV00041B/1282